FREE BOOKS & FREE STARBUCKS?

Hey, It's Mark Harrison Here!

Before you read my book, I started a new group called "Backstage Readers"

You will get all my upcoming books about self-help for FREE!

I will also be giving out FREE Starbucks Gift Card Codes once in a while to spice things up!

Just click here if your interested, I will only be accepting 57 people to be in the group.

CLAIM YOUR SPOT HERE

Click here & CLAIM YOUR SPOT HERE

https://markharrison.gr8.com

TABLE OF CONTENTS

INTRODUCTION

Somewhere around 1990, the term "emotional intelligence" was coined. However, this is a topic that has been considered since the 1930s. Many experts believe that emotional intelligence, or EQ, is more important than intelligence, or IQ. They believe that EQ is a better predictor of overall success than IQ.

In this book, we are going to explore the topic of emotional intelligence. We will start out by talking about what exactly the term "emotional intelligence" means. Then, we'll look a little at the history of emotional intelligence and why it's so important. Some experts believe that emotional intelligence is something you're born with- or you're not. However, since there are some experts who believe it is a skill that can be tested (and improved), we're going to take a look at some of the methods that can be used to measure where you are in your emotional intelligence and help you focus on the areas that you need to improve.

Moving on from that, in Chapter 2, Fundamentals for Learning Emotional Intelligence, we'll take a look at the characteristics of emotional intelligence and how you can improve your own emotional intelligence both personally and as a leader.

Since emotional intelligence is key to success in all areas of your life, we're going to take a look at relationships in Chapter 3. We're going to take a look at the four general types of relationships in your life (there are many different relationships that we have, but they will all fit into one of these categories) and why relationships are so important to us as individuals.

In chapter 4, we're going to look at some ways that you can work to improve your emotional intelligence. Finally, in chapter 5-7, we'll provide a 30-day guide to improving your overall health and wellness, which will serve to increase your emotional intelligence.

CHAPTER 1

WHAT IS EMOTIONAL INTELLIGENCE?

You know that it's essential to be able to control and (appropriately) express your own emotions- but did you know that it's also essential to be able to understand and respond to the emotions of others? Just imagine what it would be like if we lived in a world where you didn't understand when your friend was upset about something or a colleague was angry- it wouldn't be a very pleasant existence. In the world of psychology, this ability is known as emotional intelligence, or EQ, and some experts claim that perhaps this is more important than your IQ.

What is Emotional Intelligence?

The ability to perceive, evaluate, & control emotions is referred to as emotional intelligence, or EQ. Some research indicates that this is an ability that is inborn and cannot be changed. However, there is other research that indicates that perhaps this ability can be learned and strengthened.

In 1990, John D. Mayer and Peter Salovey emerged as leading researchers in this area when they defined emotional intelligence. They deemed that it was defined as "the ability to monitor the feelings and emotions of themselves and others, to distinguish them from each other, and use this information to guide their own actions and thoughts."

4 Branches of Emotional Intelligence

Mayer and Salovey developed a model identifying 4 levels of emotional intelligence:

➢ Perceiving emotions: this is the first step and, in many cases, involves understanding nonverbal cues, including facial expressions and body language.
➢ Reasoning with emotions: in this step, emphasis is put on using emotions to promote cognitive activity.
➢ Understanding emotions: emotions have a wide variety of meanings- if someone is angry, we must determine what caused the anger and what it means.
➢ Managing emotions: learning to regulate emotions, express them appropriately, and respond to the emotions of others are critical parts of EQ- and the highest level you can achieve.

Mayer and Salovey claim that the four branches of their model are arranged from the basic to the more advanced

                    EMOTIONAL INTELLIGENCE

psychological processes. That is, the first level is the fairly simple ability to perceive and express emotion, while the fourth level is being able to regulate emotions.

Outlining the History of Emotional Intelligence

While the term "emotional intelligence" was not coined until around 1990, here's a brief outline of how it came to be:

- **1930s:** the concept of "social intelligence" is described by Edward Thorndike as the ability to get along with others.
- **1940s:** according to David Wechsler, success in life is dependent upon effective components of intelligence.
- **1950s:** Abraham Maslow, and other humanistic psychologists, began describing how emotional strength can be built.
- **1975:** the concept of multiple intelligences is introduced by Howard Gardner in *The Shattered Mind*
- **1985:** "emotional intelligence" is introduced in Wayne Payne's doctoral dissertation.
- **1987:** the term "emotional quotient" is introduced by Keith Beasley in an article in Mensa Magazine. However, Reuven Bar-On claims that he used the term first in his unpublished graduate thesis.
- **1990:** Mayer and Salovey publish their article, "Emotional Intelligence" in *Imagination, Cognition, and Personality*, a psychological journal.
- **1995:** the idea of emotional intelligence is made popular after Daniel Goleman publishes his book, *Emotional*

Intelligence: Why It Can Matter More Than IQ. (We'll look at this closer in the next chapter)

Why is Emotional Intelligence Important?

While there are some experts that say EQ is more important than IQ, that does not mean that they are enemies- you can have high levels of both of them. However, the truth is that life is a social construct and without having the ability to function within this framework, intelligence is not going to get you very far. In many ways, EQ is the very essence of being human. Theodore Roosevelt understood- he said, *"No one cares how much you know until they know how much you care."*

EQ is beneficial for us in a variety of ways, from helping us to take care of our own physical and mental well-being to our ability to lead/inspire. It is our protection when it comes to resolving conflicts and it helps us to mange relationships. As you can tell, EQ truly is the driver of success in so many ways.

Of course, EQ does not only drive our personal success- but also drives our success in the workplace. About 70% of the time, people who have an average IQ will outperform someone with a high IQ. Could the reason possibly be related to their EQ?

You know that EQ and IQ are not enemies and it is possible to have both- but perhaps EQ is a better indicator of success. After all, according to the Center for Creative Leadership, around 75% of careers go off track due to emotional competencies, such as:

➢ An inability to adapt to change

- ➢ An inability to elicit trust
- ➢ An inability to handle interpersonal conflict
- ➢ Unsatisfactory leadership during times of conflict/difficulty

Your entire life can be significantly affected by your EQ- even in the workplace. After all, the workplace truly is a relational environment. Usually, they are a melting pot of various emotions, strengths, personalities, and skills. This means that EQ is fused into everything you say or do in your workplace. This is the reason why those with a higher EQ are typically able to navigate the workplace more effectively. EQ allows individuals to build/drive successful teams and to respond as required to various situations.

On the other hand, those who have a lower EQ can be disastrous to the workplace. Low EQ can present as arrogance and insensitivity or even aggression and volatility. At the very worst, it can result in a demotivated staff due to bullying and harassment. An individual with a high EQ facilitates flexibility, but those with a low EQ are inflexible and rigid- which is quite dangerous for any business.

Ideally, you would want to be able to identify EQ in candidates at the recruitment stage- but it's not that easy. An individual's IQ can be identified through their academic achievements, but EQ is not that clear- it needs to be demonstrated through references and interview performance. There are a few tests that can be used to identify EQ as you will see in the following section.

How to Measure Emotional Intelligence

When it comes to measuring emotional intelligence, some experts believe that ability testing is the best method to use. After all, intelligence is an ability and can only be measured by having people answer questions and evaluating whether or not those answers are correct. Here are some of the common tests used to determine emotional intelligence:

Bar-On's Emotional Quotient Inventory: a self-report test that is designed to recognize competencies such as interpersonal relationships, stress management, self-perception, self-expression, and decision making.

MSCEIT: an ability-based test measuring the four branches of Mayer and Salovey's EQ model.

Emotional and Social Competence Inventory: based on an older instrument, the Self-Assessment Questionnaire and involves having others who know the person rate their ability in various emotional competencies.

Now that you have a better idea of what emotional intelligence, or EQ, is and why it is so important, let's explore it a bit further. In the next chapter, we'll take a closer look at some of the fundamentals for learning EQ.

CHAPTER 2

FUNDAMENTALS FOR LEARNING EQ

Everyone has different personalities, wants, needs, and different ways of expressing our emotions. It takes cleverness and tact (especially if you want to be successful) to get through all of this- which is why EQ is so important.

In the last chapter, we learned that EQ is the ability to recognize and understand your own emotions as well as how they affect those around you. EQ also has to do with the way you see others and when you can understand how someone else is feeling it can help you manage your relationships much more effectively.

Typically, individuals who have a high EQ are successful in their undertakings. This is because they are the ones that everyone wants to work with. When an email is sent by someone with a high EQ, it gets answered. If they need assistance with something, they get it. Since they make others feel good, they typically go through life with more ease than someone who is easily angered/upset.

Characteristics of Emotional Intelligence

In 1995, Daniel Goleman (an American psychologist) wrote a book titled, "Emotional Intelligence: Why It Can Matter More Than IQ". In this book, he proposed that emotional intelligence is made up of five elements:

- **Self-awareness:** individuals how have high EQ are typically exceptionally self-aware. They have an understanding of their own emotions and are able to keep their emotions from taking over. They have confidence because they don't let their emotions run rampant and they trust their own intuition. In addition, they're willing to take a look at themselves. They know the areas they are strong and the areas they need to work on improving. Many people feel like self-awareness is the most critical piece of emotional intelligence.
- **Self-regulation:** individuals who are able to self-regulate don't allow themselves to become jealous or angry and they take the time to think before they act, so they don't make careless decisions. Some of the characteristics of self-regulation include the ability to say no, thoughtfulness, and comfort with change.
- **Motivation:** individuals who have a high level of EQ are typically motivated. They are willing to delay results in favor of being successful in the long run. They love a challenge and are highly productive and effective in the things they do.

- ➢ **Empathy:** this is the ability to identify and understand the needs, views, and wants of those around you- and many would argue that this is perhaps the second most important element of EQ. Individuals who are empathetic can recognize emotions in others, even when it's not obvious. They are able to listen and relate to others and avoid judging/stereotyping too quickly- and they always live in an open and honest way.

- ➢ **Social Skills:** this is the final sign of a high EQ. Individuals with strong social skills are easy to talk to and typically work well with others. They focus on others instead of putting the focus on themselves. They communicate well, can diffuse conflicts, and are adept at building/maintaining relationships.

Chances are you've probably already figured out that EQ is critical for achieving success in life- especially when it comes to your career. It's especially important for leaders to be able to manage people and relationships. Therefore, developing and using your own EQ is a great way to reveal the leader that's inside you.

Improving Your Emotional Intelligence

Some experts believe that EQ is something that you're born with or not. There's nothing you can do about it. However, the truth is that EQ is a skill, and just like any other skill it can be learned and developed. In addition to working on your skills in the areas listed above, consider employing the following strategies:

1. Take an honest look at yourself and how you think and interact with others. Do you jump to conclusions before you know all there is to know about a situation? Do you tend to stereotype? Try to put yourself in their shoes and be more open/accepting of their perceptions and needs.

2. Consider your behavior at work. Do you need recognition for what you accomplish? There's a lot that can be said about humility- it doesn't mean that you lack self-confidence or you're shy- it simply means that you know what you did and you can be quietly confident. Allow others to have a chance to shine instead of always focusing on how you can bring attention to yourself.

3. Take time to evaluate yourself. Consider taking an EQ quiz. This will reveal the areas that you are strong and those that need a bit of work. Accept that there's no such thing as perfect- and that includes you. Honestly look at yourself- you'll find that it just might change your entire life.

4. Analyze your reactions to stressful situations. Do you typically get upset if something doesn't happen just the way you want it to or if there's a delay? Do you put the blame on others or get upset even if it's not their fault? Being able to remain in control during a difficult situation is very valuable- both within business and in your personal life. When things go wrong or don't happen the way you planned, keep your emotions in check.

5. Accept responsibility for the things you do. When you hurt someone, make sure that you tell them you're sorry. You should never try to avoid or ignore them. most of the time,

people are happy to forgive and forget when you do what you can to make things right.

6. Before you do something, think about how it will affect someone else. If your actions are going to have an impact on someone else, put yourself in their shoes and think about how it will make them feel. If the action is unavoidable, think about how you can help them deal with the aftereffects.

Improving Your Emotional Intelligence as a Leader

What comes to mind when you think about a "perfect" leader? Perhaps you think of someone that never lets his/her temper spiral out of control, regardless of the issues that are present. Perhaps you think of someone that has earned the trust of his/her staff, listens to them, and always makes sure that he/she has all of the information before making a decision about something.

Guess what? These are characteristics of a leader with high EQ. In this section, we're going to take a look at why EQ is important for leaders and how you (as a leader) can improve your own.

1. Self-awareness

When you're self-aware, you know how you feel and how your emotions and actions can impact those around you. When you're in a position of leadership, being self-aware means that you have a clear picture of what you're good at and what you're not so good at- plus, it means you behave humbly. What are some things you can do to improve your self-awareness?

> **Practice journaling:** a journal does wonders to help you improve your self-awareness. By spending just a few minutes each day jotting down your thoughts, you'll move to a much deeper self-awareness.

> **Slow down:** when you're experiencing strong emotions, such as anger, try to slow down and examine why you're feeling that way. Keep in mind that regardless of the situation, you are in control of how you react to it.

2. Self- regulation

Leaders who know how to self-regulate rarely make decisions that are rushed or emotional, attack others verbally, compromise their values, or stereotype people. After all, at the very basis of self-regulation is remaining in control. According to Goleman, this element of EQ also involved the flexibility and commitment to personal accountability of a leader. What can you do to self-regulate?

> **Know your personal "code of ethics":** when you have an idea of what is most important to you and what you're not willing to compromise on, you won't have to think twice when you're faced with a dilemma. You'll be able to make the right choice every time.

> **Be accountable:** if your reaction is to automatically put the blame on someone else when things go wrong,

     EMOTIONAL INTELLIGENCE

you need to re-evaluate yourself. Commit to owning up to your mistakes and facing the consequences, regardless of what they are. This will help you earn the respect of those around you and you'll be able to sleep better.

> **Practice calm:** when you're faced with a challenging situation, pay attention to how you act. If you need help calming yourself, try some deep breathing exercises. In addition, take some time to write down the negative things you want to say and then rip it up and throw it out. Expressing these emotions on paper is a much better way than saying them to anyone. Plus, this will help you to evaluate your actions/reactions and make sure you're being fair.

3. Motivation

Leaders who are self-motivated are always working towards their goals and they maintain high standards of quality. What can you do to improve your overall motivation?

> Re-examine what you're doing and why. It can be too easy to forget what you love about your career, so take time every now and then to remember why you chose this career path. If you're not happy, start at the root of the problem to look at your situation in a new light. You might consider revamping your goal statements, making sure that they are fresh and energizing.

> **Know how you feel about leading:** step back and consider how motivated you really are as a leader. If

you find that you need some help in this area, there are lots of places you can find some new motivation.

> **Be optimistic:** a motivated leader is typically an optimistic leader, regardless of the difficulty they are facing. Of course, it's going to take some practice to adopt this mindset, but it truly is worth the effort.

When you face a failure or a challenge of some kind, find at least one good thing about it. Perhaps it's something small, such as meeting someone new. On the other hand, it may be something that will have a long-term effect, such as a lesson you learned. In almost every situation, if you put forth the effort, you'll find something positive.

4. Empathy

When it comes to ensuring the success of your team or organization, empathy is crucial. Leaders who are empathetic are able to put themselves in someone else's shoes. They work to develop others on their team, challenge those who are acting improperly, offer constructive feedback, and take the time to listen to those who need them. If you are interested in earning the loyalty and respect of your team, prove to them you care through your empathy. What can you do to improve your empathy?

> **Put yourself in their shoes:** it's always easy to support your own opinions, right? However, when faced with a situation, take the time to think about how other people see it.

➤ **Watch their body language:** when you're listening to someone, your body is also sending a message. Perhaps you bite your lip, shuffle your feet back and forth, or cross your arms. This shows others how you feel about the present situation, and it's not always a positive message. Learning how to read body language is an asset in a leadership role because it will help you determine how the other person truly feels- which will give you the chance to respond in the right way.

➤ **Respond to their feelings:** you've just asked your assistant to work late again- and though she agrees to, she's reluctant. Take the time to respond to her feelings. Let her know that you appreciate her willingness to work extra and that you're just as frustrated about working late. If possible, try to find a way to make it up to her, such as letting her come in late one morning or even having a day off.

5. Social Skills

A leader who does well with social skills are excellent communicators. They're open to hearing both good and bad news, and are good at getting their team to be supportive and excited. In addition, they are good at diplomatically resolving conflicts and managing change. They're typically not satisfied with letting things be, but they don't just sit back while everyone else works. They set an example. What are some things you can do to improve your social skills?

- ➢ **Learn to resolve conflicts:** a leader must have an understanding of how to resolve conflicts between vendors, customers, or team members. If you want to be a successful leader, this skill is critical.

- ➢ **Improve communication skills:** think about how well you communicate. If you find that you need some improvement, work on it. Learning to communicate well has a variety of benefits in both the business world and your personal life.

- ➢ **Learn to praise:** you can inspire your team to be loyal by simply giving praise when it's due. This is a fine art- but it's definitely worth the effort.

So, as you can see, EQ is a critical skill in both your personal and professional life- especially if you're a leader. You want to set an example for your team. You can't set an example if you're emotional and always reacting instead of being proactive and balanced.

EMOTIONAL INTELLIGENCE

CHAPTER 3

TYPES OF RELATIONSHIPS

So far, we've looked at Emotional Intelligence and why it's so important in life and in your career. Now, we're going to take a look at relationships and how Emotional Intelligence affects them. First of all, let's get started with the basics.

When you hear the word "relationship", what do you think about? There are a variety of different relationships that we can have with others, and there are four basic categories that encompass them all. These are:

- ➢ Family Relationships
- ➢ Friendships
- ➢ Casual Relationships
- ➢ Romantic Relationships

In this chapter, we're going to look at these four types of relationships and in the following chapter, we'll take a look at how you can use your EQ to build, keep, and improve them.

Family Relationships

The very first place we encounter a loving, caring relationships is through our family- or at least, we should. Of course, there are cases where family is not what we need them to be, but that is a whole other topic. In this section, we're going to take a closer look at the family relationship.

A family is a group of people that have some sort of bond, such as through adoption, blood, or marriage. Ideally, children are nurtured, respected, and grow up to care for others and build strong healthy relationships. That is, EQ is encouraged. Of course, even when you do have strong EQ skills, it's not easy to make/keep friends- but we do all have the shared goal of having strong relationships in our lives.

Your "family" is made up of your parents, siblings, and even relatives that you may not necessarily interact with on a daily basis, such as your stepparents, grandparents, aunts, uncles, and cousins. Chances are that these are the people you spend the majority of your time with and the ones that you are closest to. It is very important- but also can be very difficult- to have healthy relationships with your family members.

These days, families come in a variety of shapes and sizes. There are: traditional families, blended families, single-parent families, gay/lesbian parents, and others. Regardless of the type of family you come from, you're going to have good times and bad times. That's just the way relationships in general work.

However, there are times that families experience difficulty in their relationships due to anger, confusion, hurt, and mistrust. These emotions are all very natural and there are very few families that don't have at least a few experiences with them. Of course, when you have a high EQ, it makes these difficult times much easier to navigate. That's not to say that you'll sail right through them- but you will have the tools you need to deal with them much easier.

By making a few very simple changes in the way you look at the world around you and deal with others, it's possible to create relationships that are happier and more stable. A family should be characterized by mutual support and caring. They should be a source of lifelong support for everyone. If you have been having difficulty in your family relationships, remember that it's not too late to improve it. Even if you have a good relationship already, there are things you can do as well to keep them that way. You just need to develop some simple EQ skills.

In other types of relationships, you can take a step back and evaluate it. However, when it comes to family relationships, this is much more difficult to do. Your family may be a constant presence in your life- so when you have a difficulty or argument arise, it can seem almost impossible to deal with.

Keep in mind that communication (an important EQ skill) is the key to resolving any conflict. Make sure that you use your family to your advantage. Learn to communicate with each other, build trust and respect, and learn ways that you can establish and value boundaries.

Friendships

We all need friendships in our lives and chances are, you've always had at least one person in your life that you would call a friend. A friend is someone that you know well and think about with affection, respect, and trust. As you go through life, your friendships will begin to change. Some of them will go away while others will grow much deeper. In addition, you'll meet many more people throughout your life who will be acquaintances, but they will not all become close friends. You'll start to experience changes in your friendships over the years and this is perfectly natural- but it's not always easy.

If you're shy or unsure of yourself, it can be tough to make and keep friends. However, with some strong EQ skills, you can overcome this. The best way to meet people and make friends is to become involved in activities within your community where there are others who share your same passions and interests. Another way is to always be helpful and friendly to others.

Keep in mind that you have a right to stand up for what you believe in. You should feel like you have the freedom to express your opinions around your friends without fear of rejection or retribution. If you're worried about standing up for something, that is not a very stable friendship. After all, a true friend is willing to listen to and respect your opinions- even if they don't align with theirs. You also have a duty to listen to and respect their opinions as well.

Of course, standing up for yourself could result in some tension- but as long as you have strong EQ skills, you can deal with it. Keep in mind that you should express your own ideas while also keeping in mind how your friend feels about it. You will have a much more stable relationship when you can mutually support each other.

Here are a few tips on keeping friends (we will dig a little deeper into these in the next chapter):

➢ Encourage your friends
➢ Never tease/belittle them
➢ Cooperate with each other
➢ Compromise when necessary
➢ Always be considerate of others
➢ When you disagree, talk it over
➢ When you hurt them, apologize
➢ When they hurt you, forgive

Casual Relationships

A casual relationship is formed with those that you encounter on a daily basis- someone that is not a family member, friend, or romantic relationship- perhaps someone that you don't know yet or a teacher. Chances are, you're wondering why it's important to have a healthy relationship with someone that you don't know very well.

The truth is, every relationship starts out as a casual one. If you have an unhealthy causal relationship that lacks mutual respect, you'll likely end up with a friendship or intimate relationship that lacks respect. Regardless of how deep your relationship gets, the expectations you set at the beginning of a causal relationship don't go away.

A casual relationship can transpire on a professional level, such as medical professionals, teachers, or clergy- as well as acquaintances, such as those that you know and recognize in passing. After all, it's critical to have a healthy relationship with the professionals who serve you. Chances are, you look up to them for their skills/education, right? By showing that you respect them and learning from them, you develop critical skills that you can then turn around and apply to various situations in your other relationships.

For example, while history may not necessarily be the most interesting subject for you, your history teacher may be helpful in the future for writing a recommendation letter for college. Also, doctor visits are not the most pleasant occurrences, but your doctor can help to make sure that you remain fit and healthy.

When you show respect for the professionals you interact with, you're not only benefiting yourself, you're also benefiting your other relationships. By learning some communication skills and learning to trust those who have more experience in a particular area than you, you're on your way to becoming a more balanced member of an intimate relationship.

A casual acquaintance is a very simple relationship that is easy to maintain. When passing someone on the street that you recognize, simply acknowledging them and smiling/saying hello, you're communicating appropriately. When you portray yourself in public as friendly and polite, others will be attracted to you and you're much more likely to have healthier relationships all the way around.

Romantic Relationships

In considering the various types of relationships, it's critical to understand that its possible to have an intimate relationship with anyone. The term "intimate" describes a relationship in which you can be completely yourself with someone that you respect- and who respects you in return. This connection is an emotional one that can also be physical. It doesn't necessarily have to be in the context of a romantic/sexual relationship.

Many people are under the false belief that the term "intimate" describes a physical relationship, such as a sexual one. However, the truth is that you can have an intimate relationship with anyone that you feel close to that you can be totally open and honest with. An intimate relationship gives you the chance to grow as an individual.

Now, let's talk a little bit about romantic relationships. Unfortunately, there are situations where a romantic relationship is not an intimate one. Healthy romantic relationships are characterized by mutual respect and allow for both partners to have their own identity. In healthy romantic relationships, the partners are not only part of each other, but also able to have their own friends and interests. They're don't expect to be together all the time. Just as peer pressure can have a negative impact on a friendship, partners can overpower each other in negative ways in romantic relationships, creating instability.

Why are Relationships Important?

If you're anything like most people in the world, there are lots of things that you want to achieve in your life. You have a timeline. You want to accomplish A, then move on to B, then C, and so on. However, you should always keep in mind what your main priority is: relationships.

Here are a few reasons why your relationships should always be your top priority- nothing else should matter more than them:

1.   **A relationship fulfills your most important needs.**

What do we need more than anything else in the world? It's not achievements, money, or recognition. The most important thing we need is love. Everyone- no matter who you are- needs to be able to love and to be loved. Unfortunately, we often get caught up in so many other things that we forget about how beautiful it can be to love and to be loved. Take care that you don't allow this to happen to you. Reach out and feel how magnificent it can be to love others and to let others love you. How can you make this happen? Relationships are the only way. There's nothing else you can do to love and to love others except through relationships.

     EMOTIONAL INTELLIGENCE

2. **A relationship is where you get your most significant joy.**

Did you know that one of the most important parts of a relationship is giving. If there is no giving in a relationship, it is not genuine. Whether you're giving your money, time, attention, or a simple smile, a genuine relationship is characterized by giving. Believe it or not, giving brings great joy. Unfortunately, too many times, people get so wrapped up in themselves that they forget about the joy that comes from giving. However, life is so much better when you focus on others instead of only thinking of yourself all the time.

3. **A relationship allows you to have a lasting impact on others.**

If two people were to give you advice about something, which would you listen to: the person that you know and love or the person that you don't really know at all? You are more likely to listen to the person that you know and love, right? We always appreciate those that we love more than we appreciate anyone else. Their words go right to our hearts instead of just our minds. This is why the most effective way to have a lasting impact on other people is to build a relationship with them. Be friends with them and show them that you care about them. When you do, they will listen to and respect what you have to say.

4. A relationship gives you the support of others when you're in need.

When you're in the midst of difficulty, it helps to have others to support you. There is no one in the world that can handle everything life throws at him by himself. When you look around and your world is dark and your problem looks big, there is nothing that is more valuable than your relationships and the support they bring. Your loved ones encourage you go power through the difficulty. They will go with you into your difficult situation and share the burden with you. This will make your journey that much easier.

5. A relationship is the only thing that matters.

This was mentioned earlier, but it does bear repeating. A relationship is the only thing that truly matters. When you reach the end of your life, you're not going to be focused on your awards and achievements and you won't care if you ever became rich and famous. The only thing that you will want at the end of your life is your loved ones- those who you relationships are all that matter. We don't need to wait until that moment to realize this- we need to realize it now and cultivate our relationships.

When you understand these things about relationships, it shows that you have a high emotional intelligence.

Building, Keeping, and Improving Relationships

While it's true that many of us are highly talented and brilliant, very few of us actually work in a vacuum. This is why our ability to develop relationships with others determines our overall success in relationships both in and outside of work.

You may not realize this, but we're not born with a natural ability to develop and build wonderful relationships with other people. This is a skill, just like anything else, that we must take the time to learn and master. Everyone can learn to build better relationships by clearing their mind and practicing the following:

1. Be a great listener

We all have the desire to be heard- and understood. However, very few of us are taught how to be great listeners. Most of the time, we're too busy formulating what we want to say next, instead of really listening to what the other person has to say.

When you find yourself doing this, take a breath and correct your listening pattern. After all, when we are interacting with someone who is really listening to- and hearing- what we're saying, we want to spend more time with them and a natural bond is formed.

2. Ask the right questions

The best way to show people that we are really hearing them is to make sure that we understand what they're saying. In order to do this, we must dig deeper and ask them some questions. We must repeat back to them what they say in our own words to be sure that what we heard is what they actually said. One way to do this is to say something like, "What I heard you say was..."

When other people feel like we are making an honest attempt to understand them, they are much more likely to be open and share with us. This will deepen the relationship and put us into the category of people they can talk to and trust.

3. Pay attention to others

Think about it, you are much more likely to remember and appreciate those who ask you if everything is okay, even if you haven't said anything, right? This lets us know that they're really paying attention to us. The truth is, everyone wants that.

When you're having a conversation with someone, pay attention to their body language and facial expressions- not just their words. Pay attention to whether or not their words align with their body language and facial expressions. This opens doors to having conversations that are deeper and more meaningful- which leads to developing stronger connections and trust.

4. Remember the important things

There is nothing that is more beautiful to our own ears than the sound of our name. When you make remembering people's names a priority, you are on the road to building a relationship. Then, remembering other aspects about them continues that building process. People are going to tell you what is important in their lives- all you need to do is listen and pay attention.

EMOTIONAL INTELLIGENCE

When someone is telling you about something and their face lights up, it's obviously something that is important to them, so file this factoid in your memory. You don't have to remember every little thing about them. However, make sure that you do make remembering their name and at least one important piece of info.

There are some people who keep a small notebook of significant information on the important people in their lives so that they'll have a written record they can refer to.

5. Always be consistent and keep your emotions in check

When your emotions swing from hot to cold all the time, you're going to have a very difficult time creating relationships that are meaningful. No matter how you're feeling, you must be able to temporarily put your emotions aside in order to listen and fully engage with others who are significant in your life.

If you're dealing with some strong emotions that prevent you from being able to fully engage with the other person, you're better off letting them know what is going on instead of pretending to be there for them. Everyone appreciates it when you're open and honest with them.

6. Share your story when the time is right

We all know someone that told us their entire life story within a few minutes of meeting us, totally clueless that we had little to no interest in it. In order to build relationships that are strong, you must learn how to pace yourself and share information that is suitable and that reflects the depth of the relationship.

If you're a good relationship builder, you will show that you share the emotions of the other person by mirroring them. When you share feelings of disappointment, joy, excitement, frustration, or sorrow it helps you to form a deeper connection with others.

When it's possible, try sharing situations from your own experience that reveal you can relate to their experience. However, you must avoid overshadowing or competing with their experience. This means that you must be empathetic and sensitive to their feelings.

7. Always be confident, fun, genuine, humble, positive, and trustworthy

Individuals who build great relationships are always looking for the good in the world- and they feel good about themselves. They truly want only the best for those around them and want to see them be successful.

The atmosphere that is created from the energy of those who are upbeat and positive makes us want to spend time with them because it makes us feel good too. We know they're not going to go gossiping to everyone else about what we tell them, so we feel comfortable telling them things that we wouldn't necessarily tell anyone else. Since they are confident in themselves, they don't have to act out to get people to pay attention to them. No matter how busy they are, they make time for the people who are important to them. They are always learning and seek out opportunities for self-improvement.

CHAPTER 4

TIPS FOR IMPROVING YOUR EQ

As we have learned, emotional intelligence is what fuels your overall performance- both in the workplace and in your personal life. However, you must understand that it starts with you. From your social skills and self-control to your confidence, empathy, and optimism, learning to understand and manage your own emotions can help ensure success in every area of your life.

Regardless of the professional field you're in, whether you're managing a team of twenty or you're running a company all by yourself, realizing how well you control your emotional energy is the best place to start. After all, EQ is not something that we're taught or tested on- but it is something that we can learn. Following is a list of tips that you can use to explore your own level of EQ and learn the skills that you can implement into your daily life to improve your EQ.

Emotional Intelligence

Basically, as we've learned, EQ is how well we identify and manage our own emotions, as well as how we react to the emotions of others. It's taking the time to understand how those emotions shape our thoughts/actions so that we can have more control over our own behavior and develop the skills to manage ourselves more effectively. When we are more conscious of our emotions, we are able to grow and have a deeper understanding of ourselves, which allows us to communicate more effectively with others and build relationships that are much stronger (as mentioned in the previous chapter).

Here are eight tips that you can use to discover the foundations of your own emotional intelligence.

1. Pay attention to how you're feeling

Unfortunately, most of us have busy, hectic lifestyles and it can be easy to become disconnected from our emotions. In order to re-establish that connection, try setting a timer for several points throughout your day. When you hear the timer, take a few deep breaths and discern how you're feeling. Pay attention to where the emotion is presenting itself physically in your body and what it feels like. The more you do this, the easier it will become to practice.

2. Observe your behaviors

As you are practicing emotional awareness, take time to pay attention to your behavior as well. Pay attention to your actions when you're experiencing certain emotions and the effect that behavior is having on your daily life. You'll find that it's much easier to manage your emotions once you become more aware of how you react to them.

3. Start questioning your opinions

These days, in our hyper-connected world, it can be easy to fall into the trap of an "opinion bubble", which is a state where your own opinions are always being reinforced by others who have similar opinions. Take some time to consider the other side of the story and have your opinions challenged- even if you still believe that you're right. This will help you learn to understand others and be more open to new ideas.

4. Own your feelings

Your behavior and emotions come from you, and you alone. They don't come from anyone or anything else around you. Learning to accept responsibility for how you act and how you feel will have a positive impact on all areas of your life.

5. Celebrate the positive

One of the key factors in EQ is learning to reflect on and celebrate the positive moments in life. Typically, individuals who experience positive emotions are more resilient and have relationships that are more fulfilling, which helps them to get past adversity.

6. Don't avoid the negative

The truth is, it's just as important to reflect on negative feelings as it is the positive. By taking the time to understand where the negativity is coming from, you become a well-rounded person, which better equips you to deal with negative issues later on.

7. Always remember to breathe

You know that life throws curves sometimes and most everyone will experience some kind of stress in their lives. When this happens, in order to avoid an outburst and manage your emotions, don't forget to breathe. Take a time out. Go to the bathroom and splash water on your face. Make yourself a drink. Go outside for some fresh air. Do whatever you need to in order to remain cool and allow yourself the opportunity to get a grip on what is going on and formulate an appropriate response.

8. Know that this is a lifetime process

One thing you must consistently keep in mind is that EQ is not something that's going to happen overnight and it's not just going to be a "one-and-done" process. This is something that you will be working on for the rest of your life.

Self-awareness

One of the key elements of emotional intelligence is self-awareness. As we have said, this is the ability to recognize and understand yourself and your emotions- and how those affect other people. True self-awareness involves a realistic assessment of your own strengths and weaknesses, as well as knowing how those around you view you. This can help point out areas where you could work on improving, help you adapt, and limit wrong decisions. Following are 7 tips to help you in this area.

1. Learn some objectivity

The truth is, it's difficult to really know yourself completely and you'll find that it's next to impossible to view yourself objectively, so it's critical to get input from those who know you. Ask your loved ones what they see as your strengths and weaknesses. Be sure to ask several people and write it all down so that you can compare it. Pay attention to any patterns in their observations and don't argue with them. They may not necessarily be right, but they can help you gauge your perception from their point of view.

2. Keep a journal/diary

One of the best ways to accurately gauge yourself is to keep a journal/diary. When you first get started, take the time to write down what happened to you, how you felt about it, and what your reaction was. By taking the time to document this information, you become more aware of what you're doing and help you determine where your problems stem from. Go back over your comments from time to time and notice any trends.

3. Understand where your motivation comes from

When first starting a project, we all have a core motivation. The problem comes when adversity appears- it's hard to keep this driving force up. Too many times people will get started on a project but then lose their motivation. Take some time to evaluate where you get your motivation from and use it to spur you to your goal.

4. Take a break

There are times that we end up having an emotional outbreak because we have not taken the time to slow down and process the situation. Allow yourself to take a break and try to read, meditate, or do yoga. You might be surprised at how much a little bit of escapism helps you. Then, the next time you end up having an emotional reaction, try to take a breath before you say or do anything.

5. Admit to your emotional triggers

Individuals who are self-aware recognize and understand their emotions as they are happening. It's critical that your emotions remain flexible and you can adapt them to your situation. Of course, you don't want to deny your emotions, but you don't want to be too wrapped up in them either. Simply take the time to process them before you communicate them.

6. Predict your feelings

When you're going into a situation, take the time to reflect on it and predict how you think you're going to feel. You can maintain control of the situation by taking the time to name and accept these feelings. Instead of simply reacting to a feeling, try to choose an appropriate reaction.

7. Always trust your gut

When you're going into a situation and you're not sure which path to take, try trusting your intuition. After all, throughout your entire life, your subconscious (your intuition) has been learning the best path to take. It is the least likely to steer you wrong.

Self-Management

Once you have a grip on self-awareness and how your emotions work, it's time to get a grip on managing yourself. This means learning to be responsible for your own actions and minimizing your emotional outbursts.

1. Give yourself a jolt

One of the best ways to keep emotions in check is to remember the old saying that motion dictates emotion. So, give your body a jolt by signing up for an exercise class or channel your busy mind with a puzzle or book. Do something different. Do you know the definition of insanity? That's right, doing the same thing while expecting something different co come from your actions. You're not going to change the results until you change what you're doing.

2. Create a schedule and keep it

If you want to effectively complete your "to-do" list, then you must create a schedule and stick to it. One expert says that scheduling appointments in your calendar can be effective. Tell yourself that you're going to do Task 1, 2, and 3 by a certain date and include how many hours you expect to invest in it. By making this promise to yourself, it's much easier to make sure it gets done.

3. Eat properly

While this may sound a bit crazy, the truth is that everything you put into your body has a significant effect on your emotional state. So, making the time and effort to make sure that you maintain a balanced, healthy diet is extremely beneficial.

4. Avoid getting mad

Try funneling your emotional energy into something productive. While you've probably been told not to bottle things up, there's nothing wrong with keeping it inside if it's an inappropriate time or place to let them out. However, when you do let them out, instead of venting on something pointless, turn it into a motivator.

5. Show interest

One of the key factors in managing your emotions and yourself is to make an effort to show interest in what is going on- regardless of the subject matter.

6. Don't expect someone to trust you if you can't trust them

Trust is extremely difficult to establish- and once the trust is broken, it's that much harder to re-establish. Try to keep in mind that we're all human and we're all going to make mistakes. When you offer your trust to someone, you are extending an invitation for them to trust you in return.

7. **You decide your reactions**

One thing that we have said repeatedly throughout this book is that you decide your reaction to a situation. You can remain calm or you can overreact. There is no one and nothing else that determines your reactions.

Motivation

Following are a few tips to help you work on the motivation aspect of EQ. motivation is our inner drive to be successful and improve our overall optimism.

1. **Set personal goals**

One of the best ways to find direction and motivation is to set some personal goals for your life. Take some time to consider where you want to be and set some targets. Make sure that you keep your strengths and weaknesses in mind and make sure they are relevant to you. Finally, these goals need to be achievable and exciting. This alone will help instantly motivate you.

2. **Set realistic goals**

This one goes hand-in-hand with setting personal goals. When you set a new goal, make sure that you put real and clear aims on achieving it and accept that change is inevitable. When you achieve something, it increases your confidence. When your self-confidence increases, you are able to achieve more. It's a cycle.

3. Always think positive

One way to maintain motivation is to maintain an optimistic mindset. Instead of seeing a setback as a failure, consider it a learning opportunity. Keep in mind that the people you associate with have an effect on you- positive or negative. Therefore, when you're trying to maintain a positive outlook, it's critical that you surround yourself with positive people and avoid the negative as much as possible.

4. Never stop learning

Information and knowledge are critical for feeding your mind and maintaining your curiosity and motivation. These days, with our advanced technology, you have the chance to fuel your passions and values with the click of a button.

5. Be ready to get uncomfortable

When it comes to achieving your full potential, one of the biggest barriers is not challenging yourself enough. When you're willing to leave your comfort zone, great things can happen. So, step out of your comfort zone as much as possible. You'll be glad you did.

6. Ask for (and offer) help when necessary

When you need help, don't be afraid to ask for it- and when others need help that you can give, don't be afraid to offer it. When you watch (or help) someone else succeed, it serves as a great motivator for you.

7. Don't forget to stretch

Stretching will give you an instant motivation boost. If you're sitting at your desk, simply stand up and stretch as far as you can- holding it for 10 seconds. When you come back to your desk, you'll be in the right frame of mind and ready to get back to work.

Empathy

Empathy is defined as being able to understand the emotions of others, to understand that we are all different and have our own sets of feelings, fears, desires, and triggers. When you are empathetic, you allow the experiences of someone else resonate with yours to respond appropriately. This is a lifelong skill and critical for navigating relationships. While this is not always a natural ability, there are a few things you can do to nurture it.

1. Learn to listen

Of course, before you can even begin to be empathetic with someone, you must understand what they are saying. This means that listening is at the very foundation of empathy. Listening means that you allow them to talk without interrupting them. It means that you set aside your personal issues in order to allow yourself to absorb what they are telling you and consider their feelings before you react.

2. Be someone others can come to

Whether you're a leader or a participant, it's necessary that you are always approachable and accessible to others.

3. See their point of view

Chances are, you've heard the phrase, "put yourself in their shoes." You may have even said it a few times. The best way to gain some perspective next time a situation arises, mentally switch places with the other person and consider things from their perspective. In many cases, there really is no right or wrong, but at least maybe you can gain enough understanding to give some advice or come to an agreeable solution.

4. Be open

One of the best ways to express empathy is to truly listen to what the other person is telling you and compare it with a similar experience from your own life. You should never be afraid to open up, it could open the door to a new and lasting friendship.

5. Submerge yourself in a new culture

You've probably heard the old adage that "travel broadens your mind". Well, even in this ever-shrinking world we live in, it still holds true. Sometimes the best way to open up to others is to find somewhere new to visit.

6. Be curious about others

Individuals who have the most empathy are those who are curious about people they don't know. When we talk to people who are not within our typical social circle, we begin to learn about and even understand lives, opinions, and viewpoints that don't always align with our own. Next time you're out and about, strike up a conversation with someone- you never know what you might learn.

7. Recognize what others are saying

Another thing to remember while listening to someone is to use words and phrases that let them know you hear and understand. You can say things like, "I see" or "I understand" or something to that effect. You may even want to ask questions about what they're saying to get them to expand upon it. This lets them know that you're paying attention. However, you should only do this if you are really listening to them.

Social Skills

When it comes to emotional intelligence, social skills are those skills necessary to effectively handle and influence emotions of others. This covers a variety of abilities from conflict management and communication to meeting new people and building relationships (as discussed in Chapter 3). Social skills play a part in nearly every part of our lives from work to romance. It is a complex set of skills and requires that we use nearly everything we've mentioned so far. Here are a few additional pointers.

1. Isolate one skill to work on

To get started on improving this portion of your emotional intelligence, you need to isolate one skill that you know you need to work on. This gives you the focus you need. Goleman suggests that you choose someone that you know who is good at the skill you need to work on and observe how they behave and control their emotions, and then apply that information to yourself.

2. Put yourself in their shoes

This was briefly referenced in the empathy section- but it stands repeating. It's great advice and while we're all apt to repeat it, very few of us actually follow it. Try it out, you never know what might happen.

3. Don't forget to practice

You've heard the phrase, "practice makes perfect". This applies to social skills too. While it may sound silly, just like everything else, you won't improve if you don't practice.

4. Ditch social media

This may sound crazy in today's world, but the best way to utilize and practice your social skills is to get offline and engage face-to-face. So, instead of texting your friend about his/her problems, try suggesting that you meet for a drink or ice cream. You're not going to improve your emotional intelligence by hiding behind your screen.

5. Utilize networking

One good way to practice social skills is to attend local events to network with others. The thing about these types of events is that everyone who is attending has the same goal- to meet other people who they can help or can help them.

6. Watch your tone

You've probably said it, or at the very least it's been said to you, "it's not what you say, it's how you say it." Your tone and body language are critical and have a significant impact on how others see you. After all, it lets people know how you really feel. Once you have learned to rein your emotions in, consider how what your body is saying.

7. Get out and be social

While it sounds super simple, the truth is that the best way to increase your social skills is to get out there and use them. Consider joining a network/group that is outside of your norm. This is the best way to put all of these tips into action.

Things You Must Avoid

If you want to improve your EQ, you must pay attention and be wary of the following. These are traits that people with a high EQ very rarely display.

1. Drama

Individuals with a high EQ are able to listen, offer advice, and be empathetic for those who truly need it. However, they don't allow the lives and emotions of others have an effect on their own.

2. Complaining

Complaining implies two things:

➤ We are victims

> There are no solutions to our issues

Individuals with a high EQ very rarely feel victimized and even less often do they feel that there is no solution to what they're dealing with. Instead of searching for someone to put the blame on, they think constructively and then come up with a solution in private.

3. Negativity

Individuals with a high EQ are able to curb cynical thoughts. They are able to acknowledge that negative thoughts are just thoughts. Instead of jumping to conclusions, they rely on facts. They possess the ability to tune out or silence any negativity.

4. Focusing on the past

Individuals who have a high EQ are able to learn from their mistakes and bad choices, but instead of focusing on them, they ground themselves in the present. They don't forget the past, but they do forgive themselves for it and move on to live happy and productive lives.

5. Selfishness

While it's true that in today's society you do need to be somewhat selfish in order to get ahead- too much of it can actually result in disharmony and cause relationships to fall apart. Consider the needs of others and avoid being overly selfish.

6. Give in to peer pressure

Individuals with a high EQ don't feel compelled to follow suit just because "everyone else is doing it." They know how to think for themselves and don't conform just to make everyone else happy.

7. Being too critical

Individuals with a high EQ understand that nothing will destroy someone's morale quicker than being critical of them. Keep in mind that we are all human and share the same motivations and limitations. Be sure that you take time to understand the other person and then calmly explain to them what you would like to see happen.

In the next few chapters, we'll look at some ways that you can increase your health and happiness- which, in turn, increases your overall emotional intelligence.

CHAPTER 5

30-DAY GUIDE TO INCREASING HEALTH, HAPPINESS AND EQ

Unfortunately, when we hear the term "wellness", we assume it's something that we can't do- it's only for holistic doctors, wellness practitioners, or advanced yogis. There's no way that it's feasible for those of us who are everyday people, living our busy lives and working the daily grind. The truth is, it's a mistake to feel this way. At it's very basic level, wellness is the combination of the small daily choices we make that lead up to major, lifelong changes. Absolutely anyone can achieve wellness, regardless of whether you are a full-time working adult, a stay at home mom, or working two jobs just to make ends meet. This is not something that you need to invest a lot of time and money into. We all have access to wellness if we really want it.

In order to get you started on your journey of increasing your health, happiness- and therefore, EQ. In the next two chapters, you'll find a couple of checklists you should follow. Remember, you'll never increase your health and happiness by deciding that you're unworthy, making excuses, or sitting around wishing. This is an active decision you must make on a daily basis.

CHAPTER 6

HOW TO INCREASE YOUR HEALTH

When you feel better physically, you increase your EQ. When you're not feeling well, you're more likely to be caught up in yourself and your own feelings- and you don't always even know how to deal with them. In this section, you'll find 30 tips for increasing your health.

1. Add berries to your breakfast

Did you know that berries are packed with nutrients to fuel your body and brain? Plus, they're an amazing disease-preventative. When you eat berries with our breakfast, you'll stay fuller longer than you would if you ate cereal with dried fruit. Simply add ½ cup of your favorite berries- fresh or frozen- to your breakfast. Plus, since they're full of vitamin C, berries are excellent for kickstarting your immune system.

2. Add greens to your diet

Adding one leafy green or green veggie to one meal per day is a wonderful way to boost your health without really thinking about it. Sneak some spinach into your daily smoothie or add a cup of broccoli or green beans. Perhaps you'd rather have a salad, or some kale tossed with simple seasonings and sweet potato. There are so many options- just make sure that whatever you choose is natural and green. These foods are much more nutritious than anything else out there. They not only promote overall physical wellness, but mental wellness as well- and, like berries, protect you against a variety of diseases.

3. Drink water when you first wake up

This is still a fairly new health practice that is gaining popularity. Drinking a glass of water is critical for rehydrating your body after a night-long fast. The water helps your body wake up and is a great way to flush the toxins out of your body first thing in the morning and keeps you regular- which is necessary for your health. Keep in mind that your body is made up (and needs) more water than you might realize. Make sure that you give your body what it needs beginning first thing in the morning- even before you grab that cup of coffee.

4. Choose plain coffee and tea

As long as they're produced without pesticides, that is sustainably organically sourced, coffee and tea are two great sources of antioxidants. Both of these beverages promote heart and liver health, as well as boost your overall mental health. Of course, you'll want to leave out the milk and sugar, as that negates their benefits. In fact, in recent years, coffee is being studied for its healthy effects on cancer prevention, while tea has been considered a health remedy for years. Feel free to enjoy 1 or 2 cups in the morning, and in the afternoon (if they're caffeinated, before 3 PM).

5. Cook for yourself

When you cook for yourself at home, you are doing two things: you're putting yourself in touch with the food you're eating to keep you healthy and it helps you avoid restaurant options that someone else cooked, most likely using ingredients that are not the best for you. So, it's a good idea to simply leave out the middleman and cook at home more often- even if it means making simple dishes, such as a protein and veggie, soup, salad, macro-bowl, or a smoothie with oatmeal for a fun breakfast or dinner option. Cooking for yourself truly is one of the best things you can do for your overall health and wellness.

6. Skip the salt, use herbs

Instead of grabbing the salt shaker and using it on all of your foods, consider using herbs to flavor them. for a sweet and spicy flavor at breakfast, consider using ginger, cardamom, and cinnamon. For lunch, try turmeric, Italian seasoning, black pepper, cayenne, or sage. For diner, you might consider using thyme, pepper, garam masala, basil, or oregano. You can mix these however you want- just make sure that you're using them more often than you're using salt. After all, they offer lots of antioxidants, anti-cancer benefits, and are great for boosting your mood. In addition, since you're not using so much salt, you'll see your blood pressure decrease.

7. Ditch the excess sugar

The truth is, sugar is not part of a healthy diet. After all, sugary foods are usually heavily processed and have no nutrients. Plus, they can be addicting. So, instead of grabbing a sugary snack when you're feeling hungry, grab an orange, a handful of berries, an apple, or a banana. If you don't want fruit, consider grabbing a sweet veggie, such as carrots. When you give it the chance, your body will learn to enjoy the taste of fresh fruits and veggies. Sugar is terrible for you- it accelerates the aging process, it makes you cranky and tired, it messes with your digestion, and it doesn't fill you up. Stop eating it and you'll feel better before you know it.

8. Go for a 20 to 30-minute walk/jog

While this may sound like a challenge, the truth is it's actually much easier than you realize. Simply setting your alarm for 30 minutes earlier will give you all the time you need to get in a decent walk/jog. If you enjoy running, that's even better- but it's not necessary, especially if you're just starting out. When you get moving first thing in the morning, you provide energy to your body, increase your serotonin levels, and it will help you focus better during the day. Plus, it's a great way to increase your metabolism, which helps with weight management.

9. Spend 5 minutes every day lifting something heavy

How many times have you thought that you didn't have time to lift weights? Perhaps you have plenty of time, but it's just not something you enjoy. Whatever your situation is, here is an easy way to counter this battle. Choose something heavy- it can be a dumbbell, kettlebell, or just a heavy household item that you can grasp that you can easily pick up but has a little weight to it. Then, spend 5 minutes a day lifting it- preferably over your head and by your sides, as if you were working out your arms at the gym. You may even try to hold this item while you do some squats. Resistance training is great for improving your metabolism and your testosterone- which increases your energy and improves focus and motivation. In addition, even though it's only 5 minutes a day, it helps to strengthen your body. If you've got time, do more- but if you don't have the time, 5 minutes is enough to get results. If you can find three 5-minute increments throughout your day to do this, you've spent 15 minutes lifting weights without even realizing it.

10. Don't sit too long

While it's true that sitting is not nearly as bad as experts are telling us, it is still critical that we don't sit for long periods of time. We do need to be standing more during the day, even if it's while talking on the phone, chatting with friends, or getting up to walk a few steps every now and then while relaxing in the evenings after work. If you watch a lot of TV, don't sit there for hours doing so. If you work at a computer most of the day, consider standing while you work some or at least try to get up and move around from time to time during the day. When you sit for long periods of time, you end up more tired, your insulin levels increase, your metabolism slows down, and you end up with brain fog. Plus, sitting for too long can cause you to be in a bad mood and have an antsy nature. Your body was made to move- give it what it needs.

11. Be active during errands and commutes

When you're running errands or commuting to work, try being as active as you can. For example, if you have the option of taking the stairs or elevator, take the stairs. If you are close enough to work to walk, consider walking more often than you drive. When you live and work in a large city, this is much easier. However, those who rely on public transportation and cars to get around must keep this in mind in order to avoid sitting and being less active.

12. Stretch during the day

One of the most overlooked exercises to improve your mood is stretching. However, it has lots of benefits: it improves blood and lymphatic flow, releases muscle tension, and prevents muscle cramps. All of these lead to a healthier, happier you. Plus, stretching keeps your digestive tract working properly and keeps your muscles from getting stagnant and making you feel bad. Simply take a few moments in the morning to stretch when you first get up and again just before you go to bed at night. Just a couple of minutes spent stretching will make you feel so much better.

13. Spend time outside

Take a walk through your neighborhood or local park ever day. If you have a dog, take them with you. If you have the chance, exercise outside- it's so much more rejuvenating than walking on a treadmill indoors. Spending just a few minutes of your day being active outside is a great way to lift your mood without trying.

Spending time outdoors puts you in touch with nature- which has been proven to prevent depression and benefit your brain. Plus, it gives you the most natural source of vitamin D possible: the sun.

14. Try practicing yoga

While it's true that not everyone enjoys yoga, the benefits it brings are so amazing that it's something we should all at least try. Many people are intimidated by yoga because it feels strange or out of reach to them. Don't let this happen to you! Basically, it's just a fluid way to move your body, stretching you out, and a way to be kind to your body. Sure, an intense workout at the gym is great for pumping your muscles, but yoga is a great way to decrease the stress hormone, cortisol, in your body. This will help decrease stress throughout your day and reduce insulin spikes caused by increased cortisol. Just 10 minutes a day will make a big difference.

15. Eat for the hormone health

When we're planning out a meal or grabbing something to eat, most of us really don't think about our hormone health. However, this is definitely something we need to be doing. After all, our hormones are in control of how we act, think, feel, and treat other people. Guess what influences our hormones for the most part? That's right: diet, lifestyle, and sleep patterns. Though it's true that staying active, managing stress, and getting adequate rest does have an effect on our hormones, there's nothing that does more than the food that we eat. There are certain foods that can cause a disruption in proper hormone function and could potentially lead to anxiety, depression, and other mood disorders.

Some of the most common foods that you should be avoiding are sugar, dairy, processed foods, and gluten. Even if you're not allergic to gluten, it does have an effect on the way your brain operates and can result in hormone disorders. In addition, many dairy products have been linked to estrogen imbalance, anxiety, depression, and brain fog. One of the reasons that these foods create problems is due to their protein structures, which interfere with hormonal processes. Finally, sugary and processed foods can mess with your insulin levels and interfere with hormone functioning as well. Make sure that you're choosing whole, unprocessed foods as often as you can. Some of the best foods you can choose to give your brain what it needs are fruits, veggies, and leafy greens.

16. Spend time doing something you love on a daily basis

This can be something simple such as spending a few minutes writing in your journal, cooking your favorite meal, working on your favorite hobby, or anything else that gives you joy. When you do something for yourself every day, no matter how small, you give your serotonin levels a boost- which increases your "feel good" hormones.

17. Eat foods that are high in magnesium

Magnesium is an excellent way to combat stress- and it brings about lots of other benefits as well. Plant-based foods are high in magnesium and should be included in your daily diet to enhance your mental wellness. Some of the best ways to get adequate magnesium in your diet are: sweet potatoes, nuts/seeds, leafy greens, avocado, cacao, and bananas.

18. Choose good fats

While we're told that fats are bad and should be excluded from our diets, the truth is, there are some good fats. Healthy fats fuel a good mood and balance metabolism. In addition, healthy fats actually reduce cholesterol, increase heart health, and don't contain any of the negative effects that are associated with saturated fats from animal products. Choose things like acai fruit, almonds, avocados, cashews, chia seeds, flax seeds, hemp seeds, pumpkin seeds, raw coconut, and walnuts. Most of these also have lots of B vitamins, magnesium, and protein to increase brain health even more.

19. Stop the negativity

When you are always telling yourself that you can't do anything, will never achieve anything, or don't deserve anything, you're never going to get anywhere. Stop talking down to yourself and start talking yourself up instead. You have the power to change your entire life when you change the way you think and talk to yourself. This is one of the most important things that you can do to improve your mood and mental health on a daily basis- but it's one of the things that is most often overlooked.

20. Get plenty of B vitamins

Who doesn't want to enhance focus, promote energy and decrease stress? One of the best ways to do this is with B vitamins. Vitamin B12 is not the only one you need to think about- the other ones are important too: B3, B5, B6, and B7 are also critical for your overall health. If your diet is plant-based, you're able to easily get adequate amounts. Some of the best ways to get vitamin B are through nuts/seeds, coconut, leafy greens, root veggies, bananas, broccoli, legumes, avocados, whole grains, beans (including cacao and coffee), berries, and pumpkin. Don't get stuck eating just one though, mix them up for some variety and ensure healthy brain functioning all day!

21. Add more plant-based foods to your diet

Whether you're a vegan or not, eating plant-based foods is a great way to improve your overall mood. Research has proven that plant-based foods relieve anxiety and depression and improve overall mental clarity.

22. Spend time socializing

When we think about wellness, most of us really don't think too much about social wellness, but we should be. Even if you enjoy being alone, the fact is that we're made to be social. We're not meant to give ourselves the advantage of being social when we can. Spending time with other people can help improve mood, promote longevity, and even help relieve stress. So, make time to visit with loved ones or chat with someone in the office, at the park or at the gym. These are all excellent ways to fill your social needs daily.

23. Learn to enjoy sleep

Unfortunately, with our busy schedules, sleep is something that we've had to learn to work into our schedules. However, we should see sleep as a gift- it's just as critical for our overall health as our exercise and diet habits. Sleep is when our body detoxifies and resets itself- and prepares for the following day. When we're not getting adequate rest, we end up feeling depressed, stressed, and craving foods that are bad for us- which leads to weight gain. Some of us only need about 8 hours of sleep, while others really need about 9-10.

24. Embrace the minimalist lifestyle

While it's great to have nice things, you should never forget how much joy you'll feel from living the minimalist lifestyle. Of course, that doesn't mean you have to give all your things away and live in a box. Becoming a minimalist can be something as simple as learning how to prepare simple meals. Minimalism is the idea that sometimes less is more and it's the little things that bring the most joy. Consider going through your wardrobe and getting rid of the things you don't wear anymore. Stop going to the department store for expensive beauty products and consider using more natural options. Go through your kitchen and clean it out- sticking to whole foods that are simple to prepare. These are all great ways to simplify your life, which can make you much healthier and happier.

25. Try something new once a month

We get in our routines and we end up becoming creatures of habit. If we're not careful, we can end up just going through the motions, which makes us unhappy and bored and we could end up losing our passion for things that we care about. The best way to avoid falling into this trap is to try something new whenever possible- at least once a month. It can be something simple, such as trying a new recipe or cooking style, working in a different atmosphere, trying a new workout routine, or visiting your local farmer's market instead of chain grocery store. You'll be amazed at how good it makes you feel to try something new.

26. When you can, do something nice for someone else

When you do something nice for someone, you're not only helping them- you're helping yourself. Just as we're meant to be social, we're also meant to be giving. However, many of us see giving as a sacrifice. The truth is, when we give, we get so much in return. Of course, giving doesn't have to be related to money. It can be something simple such as making a dish for someone, sending them a card or an email, taking someone to lunch, running an errand for a friend, or letting them go ahead of you in line at the grocery store. Try being more giving and see how it makes you feel. You just may change someone's life in ways that you don't even realize.

27. Instead of taking energy from the room, bring it

Regardless of what we have going on, one of the things we must always strive to do is bring energy to a situation instead of taking it away. This means that we must always remain positive, even if our lives are not going the way we planned. When you have a positive spirit, you can make a huge difference in the lives of those around you. If we all made it a point to practice this on a daily basis, we would live in a much happier, more energetic world.

28. Each morning, take some time to be quiet

If you do your workout in the mornings, it's a great way to get some quiet time for yourself- but even if you're not, try to get at least a few minutes of quiet. This will help to decrease cortisol levels, which typically peaks first thing in the morning. Plus, it gives you time to reflect on your day before you get started. You may wish to take the time to jot down what you're thinking about, concerns, prayers, or anything else that comes to your mind. This is a wonderful, simple way to take care of yourself- then, you can focus on your day and what you can do for others.

These tips will all help you become healthier- which helps you become happier as well. In the next chapter, we'll take a closer look at some tips that can help you increase your overall happiness.

CHAPTER 7

TIPS TO INCREASE HAPPINESS

In the last section, we looked mainly at some ways to ensure overall health. While we touched on ways that you can improve your happiness, in this section, we're going to offer a few more.

1. Spend time outdoors

One of the best ways to increase serotonin levels in your brain is to spend time outdoors in the sunlight. Even just 10 minutes outside can increase your mood and help you feel focused and calm.

2. Make something

You're not expected to create a museum-worthy masterpiece- and you don't even have to share it with anyone, but spending time creating art offers your brain a distraction from the usual thoughts. In addition, it causes your neurotransmitters to create dopamine, which makes you feel good and is often referred to as the "motivation molecule".

3. Watch a live show

Most of our entertainment comes from a screen, so make an effort to see a live performance from time to time. Whether you go see a play or the opera, or your favorite band, when you're surrounded by others who are interested in the same thing, you will enjoy it that much more.

4. Go to bed early

As mentioned previously, sleep is critical to your overall well-being. When you don't get enough sleep, some of your brain activity is altered. This could mean that you have difficulty making decisions or solving problems, coping with change, and understanding/processing your emotions. The amount of sleep you need varies and may not be the same as someone else, but instead of skipping the alarm and sleeping in on days you don't have to work, try going to bed early the night before.

5. Spend time gardening

If you have a garden, spend some time weeding it, or buy some new seeds/plants. Many mental health professionals recommend gardening for those who have mental health issues because it has so many benefits. It serves as exercise, it gets you in touch with nature, and it's meaningful and creative.

6. Talk to your friends

Of course, when you talk to your friends- make sure you're reaching out to the positive ones. Reach out to those that you enjoy spending time with and leave you feeling connected, inspired, and enriched. When you surround yourself with people who are positive, you're much more likely to share their outlook.

7. Get sweaty

Don't let this one intimidate you. You are not expected to do an intense, hour-long workout. Just spend 5 minutes running or go out bowling with your friends. One of the best ways to improve your mood is to do something that gets your blood pumping.

8. Be crafty

Spend some time doing embroidery, cross-stitching, making some pom-poms, or anything else you enjoy. In addition, consider learning something new- this will increase your feelings of self-worth and you may even meet some new people if you take the time to join a handicraft group.

9. Try meditation

Previously, it was suggested that you spend time in the quiet before getting your day started. You might want to use this time to meditate. This is a great way to change your brain chemistry. Meditation is all about being in the present moment and helps to increase your resilience against the hardships of life.

10. Do yoga

The practice of yoga dates back more than five millennia and studies have revealed that it is effective not only for improving physical health, but mental health as well. Studies show us that the GABA levels in the brain spike after just one hour of yoga. There are lots of different levels and types of yoga, so it should be easy to find one that fits you, even if you don't think you're a "natural."

11. Work on a puzzle

One of the best ways to relieve stress is to find an old jigsaw puzzle with missing pieces or a brain-training app. These engage your mind a way that is light-hearted, and not so serious. Plus, if you complete the puzzle, you get a bonus sense of accomplishment, which increases your self-esteem and self-confidence.

12. Listen to music

When you're feeling blue, instead of cranking up that sad song, find something that is upbeat. Studies have proven that happy music can improve your mood as well as benefit your body. Music affects your autonomic nervous system, which controls your heartbeat, blood pressure, and limbic system, which is responsible for your emotions.

13. Play with your pet

Scientists have proven that stroking a pet relieves anxiety and stress. So, when you're feeling bad, find a furry friend to spend some time with. Then, see how you feel after. If you're still skeptical, ask people in hospitals, care homes, or areas that are dealing with a disaster, how they feel after receiving affection from therapy animals.

14. Cook something from scratch

For a long time, avid cooks have acknowledged the therapeutic power of spending time in the kitchen. It a lot like meditation, only with cooking you have the promise of something good to eat at the end. If possible, feed someone else too- it will not only increase your happiness, but make them happy as well.

15. Spend some time reading

A 2008 study revealed that spending some time reading fiction can enhance your mind and help you develop the skills needed to understand the mental states of others. This will better equip you to navigate complex social relationships- which brings you to a happier state of being.

16. Find a podcast and listen

One of the best ways to escape from the frustrations and irritations of your daily commute is to find a podcast- there are thousands of them available. Learning something new is at the very core of our psychological well-being. Learning new things increases our confidence. After all, as humans, we have an innate desire to learn and progress, which is what psychologists refer to as "mastery".

17. Clean up

Cleaning is a great way to not only remove clutter, dust, and dirt from your physical environment, but also to remove any negative energy and emotions. When your environment is clean, you'll be much happier and more relaxed.

18. Physically touch someone

According to the experts, skin-to-skin contact floods our body with oxytocin and other feel-good endorphins. Whether you hold hands, hug, or get a little frisky between the sheets, find someone you can be physical with.

19. Take a bath/shower

Taking the time to run a bath with bubbles, oils, and candles and soaking the day away or just simply jumping in the shower for five minutes before work has been shown to have a positive effect on mental well-being.

20. Don't procrastinate

You should never put off for tomorrow what you can get done today. When you can cross something off of your "to-do" list, especially if it's something you've been putting off, it can give you a sense of relief and accomplishment. You may even find the motivation to keep going on another task that you've been putting off, which will deepen your sense of relief and accomplishment.

21. Journal

Taking time at the end of the day before going to bed to write everything down can help you avoid overthinking things. Plus, it gets it all off your mind, which means you can sleep without worrying so much.

22. Dress up

You don't have to wait for a special occasion to dress up. Take the time to look your best for yourself. Be in control of how you present yourself. Don't feel ashamed for putting on your favorite dress to go grocery shopping.

23. Learn something new

Learning a new skill increases our sense of self-worth and self-confidence, plus it keeps us curious. Find something to do that takes you out of your comfort zone, such as learning a new language online or joining a choir. You'll be glad you did.

24. Treat yourself

Just as you don't have to wait for a special occasion to dress up, you don't have to wait for a special occasion to treat yourself. Whether you treat yourself to a pastry from your favorite bakery on a daily basis or you save up for a month or more for something special, don't neglect yourself.

25. Grooming

When you feel good on the outside, you feel better on the inside. So, consider putting on that bold lipstick or nail polish, get your hair done, or get a spray tan.

26. Cultivate gratitude

These days, it seems like everyone is always complaining. One way to cultivate gratitude is to get a gratitude journal/log. Then, take a few moments every day to reflect on your blessings. This will help you see that perhaps it's not nearly as bad as you might think.

27. Make a list of the things you love about yourself

The truth is that relationships- and even family- are going to come and go but you're going to be stuck with yourself for life.

Therefore, you might as well get used to it. Take some time to practice self-love and write down all the reasons you're so amazing.

28. Share secrets with someone

You have likely heard the saying, "a problem shared is a problem halved", right? Well, while there's no guarantee that your problem will be halved, sharing something you've been concerned about is a great way to ease your burden. The person you're confiding in may be able to provide a new perspective and help you sort through how you really feel about it.

29. Help someone else

Whether you volunteer on a regular basis or you perform some random act of kindness, giving has been proven to lead to personal growth and lasting happiness. After all, it's always better to give than to receive, right?

30. Visit somewhere new

Traveling and discovering a new place always makes people happier. You may find a new neighborhood in your area or you might take a backpacking excursion across the world, but finding new places helps you realize how beautiful the world can be.

These tips can help you increase your happiness- which will, in turn, increase your emotional intelligence.

CHAPTER 8

PRACTICING EQ

In 2017, the World Economic Forum released a report on the future of jobs, taking a look at the employment, skills, and work force strategy that we will see by the year 2020. Here's where things get pretty interesting. They asked some of the Chief Human Resource officers from various global companies what they see as the top 10 job skills that workers will need to thrive by the year 2020 in light of the fact that automation and artificial intelligence is on the rise.

Below, we'll take a look at the differences between skills needed in 2015 versus skills needed in 2020.

Here are the top 10 job skills needed in 2015:

- Complex problem solving
- Active listening
- Service orientation
- Negotiation
- Coordinating with others
- Quality control

- ➢ People management
- ➢ Creativity
- ➢ Critical thinking
- ➢ Judgement and decision making

Here are the top 10 job skills anticipated to be required by 2020:

- ➢ Critical thinking
- ➢ Coordinating with others
- ➢ Complex problem solving
- ➢ Negotiation
- ➢ Cognitive flexibility
- ➢ Service orientation
- ➢ Emotional intelligence
- ➢ Creativity
- ➢ Judgement/decision making
- ➢ People management

As you can see, there are two new skills on the list for the year 2020 that will be critical to have. One of these is cognitive flexibility. This really does make sense because superior customer service will require agility and must be personalized and conversational.

However, did you pay attention to the other new skill that appears on the list for the year 2020 that wasn't around in 2015? That's right: emotional intelligence.

Just like cognitive flexibility, EQ requires that you actually take time to contemplate and explore the needs of people from a human-centered angle as opposed to running headlong into solving the problem from a technological point of view.

According to EQ expert, Harvey Deutschendorf, the thought that EQ has become a predictor of success on the job, even more than technical ability, has been increasing over the past few years. He offered some statistics from a CareerBuilder survey in 2011 of over 2,600 hiring managers and HR professionals:

- 71% of them valued high EQ over high IQ
- 75% said they would be more likely to offer a promotion to an individual with high EQ
- 59% said they would not hire someone who had a high IQ if they had a low EQ

There are several reasons why companies are now placing high value on employees with a high EQ. Individuals who have a high EQ understand and work with other, they listen well, they are open to feedback, they are more empathetic, and they make decisions that are more thoughtful and thorough.

Tips for Practicing EQ

Following are nine practical tips that you can use on a daily basis to practice emotional intelligence.

1. Clear your mind- acknowledge what you think and feel

When you take the time to acknowledge how you feel, you are bringing together your cognitive and emotional self, which research has proven is a great way to decrease the intensity of emotional reactions. When you stop and acknowledge, you will notice your mind feels much clearer.

1. Ask yourself if you are feeling open or closed

When you are feeling compressed, deep belly breathing can help release your muscles. Take a deep breath and allow your shoulders to relax and open. As you fill your body with air, this physiological expansion will influence your mind and your emotions, increasing openness and reducing stress levels. This will allow you to make choices that are much more positive and powerful.

2. Ask yourself three questions of optimism

Stop and ask yourself the following:

A. Do I think this situation is permanent/won't get better?

B. Do I feel this situation is pervasive/changing everything?

C. Do I believe there is nothing I can do about this situation?

Then, take a step back and try to find some evidence for what you're thinking. If you find that your thoughts are inaccurate, fight them and actively make the decision to choose thoughts that are active, positive, and realistic.

3. Focus on what you have control over

When you do have a setback- and you will, we all do- take the time to separate the different parts of the situation that you can control versus those you have no control over. Then, put your focus on those things that you can have some control over and you'll find that you're much more confident about overcoming your setback.

4. Pause for six seconds

When you find that you're feeling upset and/or frustrated, before you say something that you're going to regret, take six seconds to think about the costs and benefits of saying or doing that. When you think about the consequences, you will be much more careful about the choices that you make, which means you'll make choices that are much more advantageous for you.

5. Find something that is impossible to do- and practice it

While this may sound silly, it really is a great mental switch. Try saying "I can't"- then, turn around and say "I can't yet". Notice the emotional experience between the two. The first one is a wall- it stops you from going any further. However, the second one is a door- it allows you the possibility to keep going and learn.

6. Be compassionate to everyone you encounter

Engage in a positive conversation with your taxi driver, the cashier at the grocery store, the mailman, etc. When you walk past someone on the sidewalk, say hello and smile. If you're talking with someone, ask them meaningful questions and really take the time to listen to what they say.

7. Take two

When you're feeling overwhelmed, take two minutes to take some deep, calming breaths and relax. Then, think about the problem that you're facing and write down two potential solutions.

8. Share what you feel

Be open to chances to share how you feel and ask for feedback from others. You can also create your own opportunities to do this. This will help to clear the air of any potential issues within your relationships.

These are all great ways to practice EQ on a daily basis.

We've spent some time going through the concept of Emotional Intelligence and how it impacts our lives in so many ways. We have learned that it is a critical factor to success in all areas of our lives. Now, before we close, let's take a look at how you can know if you are emotionally intelligent- and how much work you'll need to do if you're not.

How Do You Know If You Are Emotionally Intelligent?

When the idea of Emotional Intelligence first appeared, it was the missing link in an interesting finding: individuals who had average IQs would outperform those with higher IQs approximately 70% of the time. This really messed with the assumption that IQ was the only way to predict an individual's success.

Many years of research have revealed that EQ truly is the critical factor that sets the higher performers ahead of the pack. According to experts, there is such a strong link between EQ and performance that around 90% of top performers have high emotional intelligence.

As we have said, EQ is that intangible thing inside all of us that has an effect on how we:

➢ Manage our behavior

> Navigate social complexities
> Make personal decisions to affect positive results

Despite the fact that EQ is extremely significant in our lives, the fact that it is intangible means that it is hard to measure- and on top of that, if you're lacking, it's hard to know exactly what you need to do to improve.

Of course, you can always take a test that has been scientifically validated- but these types of tests typically are not free. So, we have some insights that will help you see if you have high EQ.

1. Strong emotional vocabulary

Everyone experiences emotions, but there are only a few that can accurately name them as they are happening. Research has proven that only around 36% of people can do this, which is a problem because emotions that are not labeled often end up misunderstood, leading to actions with are counterproductive and choices that are irrational.

Since they are able to understand them, individuals who have a high EQ are able to master their emotions. They use a wide variety of vocabulary to describe their feelings. While most people might describe themselves as feeling "bad", an emotionally intelligent individual can determine whether they feel "anxious", "frustrated", "irritable", or "downtrodden". The most specific the word you use, the more insight you have about the emotion you're experiencing, what led to the emotion, and what you can do about it.

2. Curious about others

Regardless of whether an individual is an introvert or an extrovert, if he/she is emotionally intelligent, they are curious about everyone. This curiosity is attributed to empathy, which is one of the most important portals to a high EQ. The more concern you have for others and what they're going through, the more curious you are going to be about them.

3. Embrace change

Individuals who are emotionally intelligent are willing to be flexible and adapt to varying situations. They understand that fear of change can be paralyzing- and a serious threat to their overall happiness and success. They are always seeking change that is waiting right around the corner and they formulate a plan of action if the changes take effect.

4. Know strengths and weaknesses

Individuals who have high emotional intelligence don't only understand their emotions, they also know what they're skilled at and what they're not so good at. In addition, they're aware of who and what pushes their buttons and who and what enables them to be successful. Individuals with a high EQ know their strengths and how to use them to their full advantage, while keeping their weaknesses from getting in the way.

5. Good judge of character

Most of emotional intelligence is about social awareness- that is, the ability to read other people, understand what they're going through, and what they're about. This skill makes individuals with high EQ a good judge of character. Other people are no mystery. You understand what they're about and their motivations- even those that are not clear.

6. Difficult to offend

Individuals who have a high EQ have a strong handle on who they are and therefore, it's quite difficult for anyone to say/do something that gets to them. Individuals who are emotionally intelligent are open-minded and self-confident, so their skin is pretty thick. Chances are, they may even laugh at themselves or let other people make jokes at their expense because they are able to draw the line between degradation and humor.

7. Know how to say no

When an individual has high emotional intelligence, they know how to apply self-control in every situation. They know how to avoid impulsive actions and delay gratification. Research performed at the University of California at San Francisco revealed that the more difficulty an individual has saying no, the more likely they are to experience depression, burnout, and stress. While it's a major self-control challenge for many people to say "NO", it is a powerful word that you should not be afraid to use. However, there comes a time when you have to say no- and when that time comes, individuals who are emotionally intelligent avoid saying things like "I'm not sure" or "I don't think I can". They say the word "NO" and mean it. When an individual says no, it honors their existing commitments and allows them to have the opportunity to fulfill them.

EMOTIONAL INTELLIGENCE

8. Let go of mistakes

Individuals who have high EQ distance themselves from the mistakes they make, without forgetting about them. Since they distance themselves from their mistakes, but still close enough for reference, they can adjust their behaviors/actions for success in the future. It requires a cultivated sense of self to walk the tightrope between remembering and dwelling on mistakes. When you overthink your mistakes, you become gun shy and anxious. On the other hand, when you completely push them out of your mind, you are much more likely to repeat them. The key to balance is in your ability to turn your failures into opportunities for improvement. This means that you're much more likely to get right back up every time you fall down.

9. Give without expecting anything in return

When you're spontaneously given something, and the giver doesn't expect anything in return, it makes an impression, doesn't it? For example, let's say that you have a conversation about your favorite book with someone and then a month later, when you see them again, they have the book for you. An individual who is emotionally intelligent is constantly thinking about others, so they build strong relationships.

10. Don't hold grudges

Those nasty emotions that come along with holding a grudge are a stress response. All you have to do is think about the event and your body goes into fight-or-flight mode, which is a survival mechanism forcing you to stand up and fight or run away when you're faced with a threat. When there's an actual threat, this reaction is critical to your survival- but if the threat is ancient history, holding on to the grudge wreaks havoc on your body and over time, can have devastating effects on your health.

Researchers at Emory University have determined that holding onto stress results in high blood pressure and heart disease. When you hold a grudge, you're holding on to stress and individuals who are emotionally intelligent understand how to avoid this. They know that letting go of grudges gives you an immediate release of stress and can also improve your health.

11. Neutralize toxic people

Most people find that dealing with individuals who are difficult can be exhausting and frustrating. However, individuals with a high EQ are able to control their interactions with toxic people by making sure to keep their feelings in check. When a situation calls for them to deal with a toxic person, they take a rational approach to the situation. They take the time to identify their own emotions and don't allow frustration or anger to add fuel to the fire. In addition, they take the time to consider the other person's viewpoint and can find common ground and a solution to the issue at hand. If a situation does happen to derail, an emotionally intelligent individual can just let things go and not let the toxic person bring them down.

12. Don't seek perfection

An individual who has high emotional intelligent know that there's no such thing as perfection, so they don't set their sights on it. By our very nature, human beings are fallible. When you make perfection your goal, you will constantly be left with a nagging feeling of failure that makes you want to decrease your efforts or completely give up. You lament your failures and think about what you should have done differently. This keeps you from being able to move forward, excited about your achievements and your future accomplishments.

13. Count your blessings

You've heard that you should count your blessings, but that's not just the right thing to do- it can also give you a mood boost by reducing the level of cortisol in your body- some studies claim a 23% decrease. Data from research done at the University of California in Davis revealed that individuals who cultivate an attitude of gratitude on a daily basis will have an improvement in their energy levels, mood, and overall well-being. It is believed that lower cortisol levels play a significant role in this.

14. Disconnect

Taking time to go "off the radar" is a sign that you have a high EQ because it allows you to keep control of your stress and to live in the moment. By making yourself available to work 24 hours a day, 7 days a week, you open the door for a constant stream of stressors to come your way. On the other hand, forcing yourself to take time off, gives your mind and your body a break. Studies have proven that taking a break from emails can be beneficial. While technology is a wonderful tool, the problem is that it allows for constant communication and you're expected to be available 24 hours a day, 7 days a week. It's almost impossible to enjoy time off work when you get an email that can potentially cause stress can come through at any moment.

15. Limit caffeine intake

When you drink copious amounts of caffeine, it triggers an adrenaline release, which is what causes your fight-or-flight response. This mechanism ignores rationality in favor of a quick response to make survival a priority. It's a wonderful thing when you have a wild animal chasing you- but when you have to respond to a curt email, it can be a bit of a disadvantage. Caffeine causes your body and brain to go into a hyper-aroused state of stress, which means that your emotions are in charge. The long half-life of caffeine also make sure that you stay in this state as it takes it's time to get out of your body. Individuals with high EQ understand that caffeine is bad for them and they don't overdo it.

16. Get enough sleep

When it comes to managing your stress levels and increasing your emotional intelligence, it's hard to exaggerate the importance of sleep. Sleeping allows your brain the time it needs to recharge, go through the memories from the day and either storing or discarding them (which causes dreams), so that you wake up clearheaded and alert. Individuals who have high EQ understand that when they don't get enough sleep, their memory, self-control, and attention suffer, so they make it a high priority to get enough.

17. Stop negative self-talk

The more you ponder negative thoughts, the more power they have. In most cases, our negative thought patterns are just that- thoughts. They are not facts. When you feel like something is always or never happening, your brain naturally perceives threats of the frequency or severity of an event. Individuals who are emotionally intelligent are able to separate these thoughts from facts so that they can escape the negative thought cycle and keep moving toward a new and positive outlook.

18. Don't let anyone put limits on your joy

When you get your sense of satisfaction and pleasure from what other people think, then you give them power over your happiness. You are no longer in charge. When an individual with a high EQ feels good about something, they don't let the opinions or snide remarks from anyone else take that satisfaction away from them. While it's almost impossible to not react to what other people think of you, you really don't have to compare yourself to them and you can always just take what they think with a grain of salt. This way, regardless of what other people think or do around you, your self-worth comes from inside.

Now that you know how to determine whether or not you have a high EQ, you know where you need to start to improve yourself. Consider the information you received in this book and do with it what you need to. We could all benefit from some EQ in our lives- it helps us function well within society and helps us to interact with each other without too many issues.